Before writing

Imagine a world without writing! No books, no newspapers, no comics, no signs, no labels, no diaries – our world would be so different. Yet there was a time when writing hadn't been invented – and when it was invented it looked very different from our writing today.

So, what was there before writing and how do we know?

First, we have to think about why people wanted to write things down. The answer is to communicate – to 'say' something to others like I am a hunter, Your grain ration is one bushel, I have bought ten sheep from you or I am a great king.

Before writing, people did communicate many things in ways other than talking, but they used pictures or tokens and kept records with the help of clay tags and labels made with seals.

The signs on this ancient Mesopotamian clay tablet mean **10 sheep.**

This much more elaborate clay seal was made in Mesopotamia about 1500 years later.

ACTIVITY BOX

1 Write down some reasons for writing! See if you can think of at least ten.

2 Cut out a picture from a newspaper or magazine which you like or find interesting. Write some headlines to go with your picture. Make each headline different! You can show people how writing communicates with us – it gives us meaning.

In Mesopotamia, the earliest permanent settlements existed before 8000 BC – that's over 10 000 years ago – and these communities developed ways, other than talking, to communicate and to record the life they were leading.

By around 5500 BC, the farmers in Mesopotamia used clay seals to show the ownership of animals, pots and tools. When one herdsman sold his animals he kept a record on a clay tag.

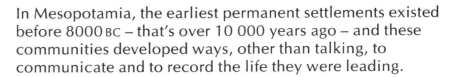

The map on page 2 shows you where Mesopotamia was.

The second question was How do we know? Well, we find out through ancient objects, like pots and seals. We also learn through later societies writing down what they thought about other groups and by the Oral Tradition (which means the spoken history).

Writing first appeared, so far as we know, more than 5000 years ago in Mesopotamia. People needed to record such things as buying and selling goods or giving out rations of grain. True writing extended the range of records that could be kept.

The earliest surviving examples of writing are **pictographic** – this means simple pictures were used to represent things like livestock, barley and other goods, or numbers. These pictures were drawn on pieces of clay which had been specially prepared.

Therefore, our first evidence isn't stories or notes but economic documents.

This clay tag means **10 goats**

This table records the delivery of barley and grain to a Sumerian temple. It is written in ancient **cuneiform** writing (see page 3)

ACTIVITY BOX

1 Make up pictographs for six things you might buy in a supermarket. Swop yours with a friend and see if you can write down the names of the things. Remember, you mustn't use any letters and don't make them too obvious!

2 Use an atlas to list the modern names of the countries shown on the map. You might find the borders of the countries have changed, but be as accurate as you can.

3 Make a **rebus** of your name or a friend's name – here's a clue to what rebus means:

 = Caroline

  = Sunil

World map showing places where evidence of early writing exists

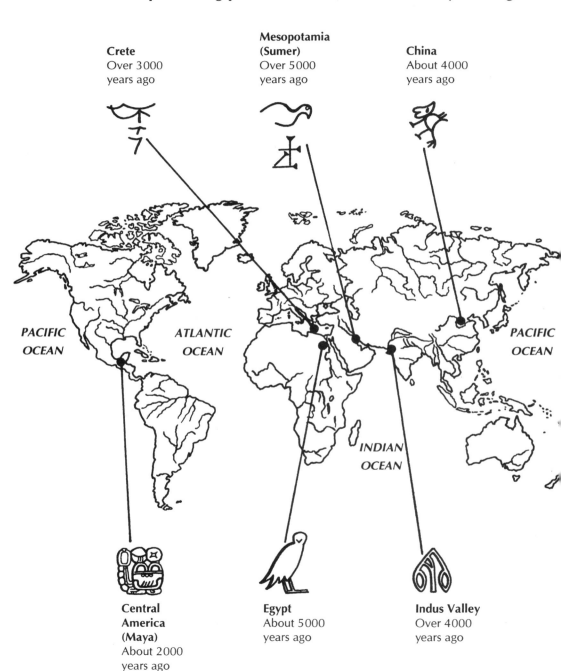

Crete
Over 3000 years ago

Mesopotamia (Sumer)
Over 5000 years ago

China
About 4000 years ago

PACIFIC OCEAN

ATLANTIC OCEAN

PACIFIC OCEAN

INDIAN OCEAN

Central America (Maya)
About 2000 years ago

Egypt
About 5000 years ago

Indus Valley
Over 4000 years ago

Sumerian cuneiform tablet, recording details of fields and crops (about 3300 BC).

Ancient Egyptian hieroglyphs, recording part of the Egyptian calendar.

Indus Valley seals, about 2500 BC. The writing may be the names of merchants.

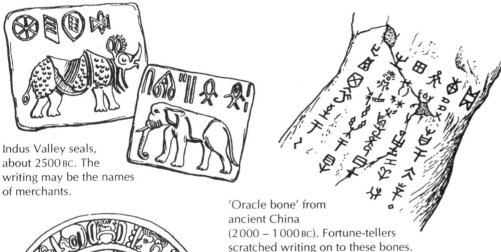

'Oracle bone' from ancient China (2000 – 1000 BC). Fortune-tellers scratched writing on to these bones.

A stone marker from a Mayan ball-game court, AD 650. The **glyphs** around the edge

Tablet from Knossos, Crete, with Linear B text. It records animals kept by the rulers of the palace. About 1450 BC.

What happened next?

Over many years people got to know the pictographs very well and started to make them simpler. They were less like elaborate drawings so they were easier to write.

The next really important thing that happened was that in Mesopotamia people began to use the pictographs to represent sounds – we call these **phonetic signs**.

This writing uses signs for sounds and also uses some of our modern alphabet.

Meet at Woodbridge today

and here it is simplified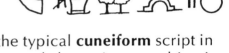

The phonetic signs became the typical **cuneiform** script in Mesopotamia. The signs were made by various combinations of wedges. The Sumerians mostly wrote the wedges on clay tablets and they used more straight lines than curved because straight lines were easier to impress on the clay. To make the marks, they used a length of reed whose tip had been cut off straight so it made wedge shaped marks. The other end of the reed was rounded and used to make round impressions.

Cuneiform means wedge shaped.

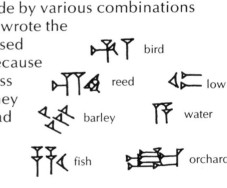

Cuneiform writing from Assyria

ACTIVITY BOX

1 Make up a code using phonetic signs and send a secret message to someone. See if they can crack the code – give them a few clues!

2 Make a square of plasticine and try writing some cuneiform signs.

How and when were pictures and symbols used in the past?

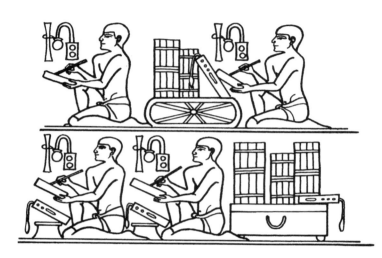

About 5000 years ago, ancient Egyptian scribes were also drawing pictures to represent man-made and natural objects. But this was not just 'picture writing' – some of the signs represented sounds as well, just as we learnt on the last page.

Not everyone could read and write in Egypt, or in Mesopotamia. Scribes were trained for this and their work was considered to be very important. Egyptian scribes wrote on papyrus rolls made from reeds which grew along the Nile River. Unlike the Sumerians, who used a reed and a clay tablet, the Egyptians used a brush and ink to write on the papyrus, and so they could draw any shape easily.

This early form of Egyptian script is called **hieroglyphic** writing.

Hieroglyphs were also used a great deal in temples where they were often carved in stone.

It was slow and difficult to write hieroglyphs so, for quicker everyday use, people soon began to use a simpler version called Hieratic writing.

ACTIVITY BOX

1 Invent your own 'hieroglyphs' for these words: BASKET, WATER.

2 Try making a 3D 'hieroglyph' in clay or plasticine or 'junk' materials.

In Central America...

Has the world come to an end and been re-created? Well, the ancient Maya peoples who lived in southern Mexico, Guatemala and Belize believed that the world had been created and destroyed at least three times. The last cycle of creation began on 13 August 3114 BC – that's about 5000 years ago. How do we know? Because with the invention of Maya hieroglyphic writing, these ancient people recorded a complicated and very precise calendar. They also recorded names, birth dates, marriages, royal coronations, wars and the deaths of ruling lords and ladies. Maya glyphs often show birds, animals, people and objects from the Maya world.

Day signs

Month signs

Numbers

1   8   10

It seems that the Maya did not use glyphs to record trading activity, buying and selling, like the Mesopotamians. They wrote about their history and rituals

In China...

Early forms of writing were also developed in China around 1500 BC, about 3500 years ago. Chinese characters first appeared on bones, tortoise shells and on cast bronze vessels dating back to the Shang dynasty (about 1250 BC). They often named the person or clan who owned the vessel and from these simple beginnings the complex Chinese script developed.

The Chinese system of writing has over 50 000 symbols or characters which represent things, ideas or sounds. The system has changed very little since it was first developed, and so people today can still read some of the old texts.

Korean and Japanese people also use Chinese characters to write with, so they can read each other's writings even though their spoken languages are different.

Some of the oldest written records in China were discovered written on the shoulder blades of oxen. These date from about 1300 BC. Writing has also been found on silk, pottery, wood, tortoise shells, bamboo and stone.

Fortunately, people in China today only need a few thousand characters to use in their everyday life!

A **calligrapher** in ancient China (see page 6)

sun

moon

bright
(sun & moon)

bird

tree

Examples of old and modern
Chinese characters

A **calligrapher** in ancient China (see page 6)

ACTIVITY BOX

1 List all the different types of materials you can think of which have writing on them. Think particularly of things at home or in school.

   Draw two examples from real life as accurately as you can.

2 Try to write a short story using signs instead of words. How many do you need?

What did people write on and what did they write with?

If you've been reading through this book you will already know that people wrote on many different types of surfaces in the past. If you're not sure or have forgotten you can go back and find out when you come to do the activities on the next page.

Here's some more information about Chinese writing implements.

For the past 2000 years, Chinese painters and **calligraphers** have used pliable brushes and an ink block to put black ink and other water-based pigments on to silk or paper.

The brushes were made of deer, goat, rabbit or wolf hair and were often fixed into a beautiful holder when not being used. Holders could be made of wood but also of more expensive materials such as lacquer, ivory and porcelain.

The inks were made of pine soot and animal glue moulded into sticks and cakes. The dried ink was mixed with a small amount of water on the slab which was made from stone or fired clay.

During the 10th century AD the brush, paper, ink and ink slab were known as The Four Treasures of the Scholar's Studio. Writing was more than just a way of recording or communicating information. It had become a work of art.

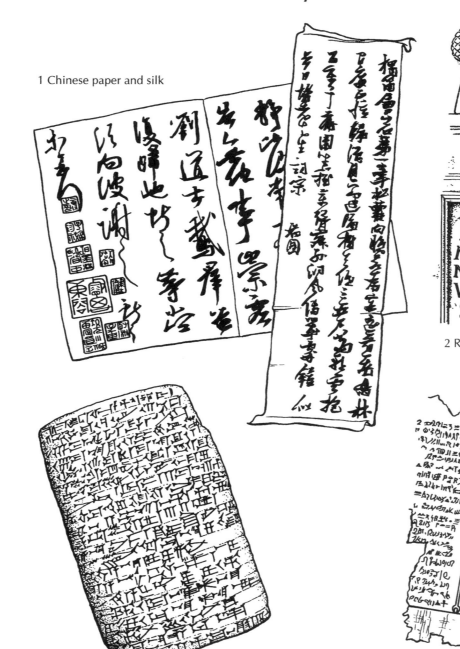

1 Chinese paper and silk

2 Roman stone monument

Paper is the main material we use to write on now. It was first used by the Chinese in the 1st century AD. They made it from linen rags which were soaked in water and then heated up to form a pulp. This mixture was poured through bamboo matting which acted as a sieve. The fibres that didn't drain through were left to dry and became paper.

Before paper was available, people used other materials that were cheap and easy to find.

ACTIVITY BOX

R	A	C	E	H	J	K	M	P	R	S	B
E	F	E	L	T	T	I	P	T	D	Y	L
P	Z	O	B	A	F	G	I	L	R	M	A
A	N	T	U	O	Q	W	X	C	A	H	C
P	E	N	K	N	R	T	Z	D	C	G	K
L	O	I	W	A	T	E	J	P	H	S	B
Y	B	O	F	I	N	A	Q	X	A	V	O
U	D	P	P	E	N	C	I	L	L	H	A
L	P	L	T	X	B	F	J	N	K	N	R
R	U	L	Z	A	C	E	G	K	P	I	D
C	R	A	Y	O	N	Q	O	M	W	E	Y
U	S	B	R	U	S	H	U	A	S	R	N

1 Look at the pictures on these pages. Match up the writing implements to the surfaces. Now write a sentence about who used the implements and, if you can, when they were used.

2 Use a dictionary to look up these words and write down a definition – but only if you understand what you're writing!

CALLIGRAPHY, PIGMENT, IMPLEMENT (the noun, not the verb).

3 Do the word search using the pictures to help you.

4 Try some different writing implements and materials. What will write on a plastic bag? What can you use to write on a block of plasticine? Try your own experiments.

Who used the first alphabets?

Do you remember learning your alphabet? It's one of the first things we do at school, or at home. When you were very small you might have called it 'knowing your sounds'. That is what the alphabet is – the individual sounds of your language.

You have already read in this book about pictograms. In Egypt and Mesopotamia, those pictograms came to stand for sounds. These sounds were **consonants** and **syllables** (in Egypt) and syllables (in Mesopotamia). A syllable is a sound like ba, bab, be, bi, bo, bu; or da, de, di, do du ... Think about how many different syllable sounds there are and you can imagine how many different signs you'd need to write them all down. It isn't surprising that only a few scribes could master writing in Mesopotamia.

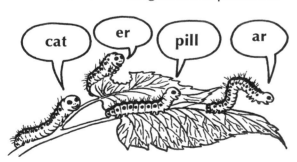

A syllable is a **vowel** attached to one or two consonants. Do you know the difference between vowels and consonants? Just in case you are not sure, here is a reminder: English vowels are the sounds of a, e, i, o, u. The

---

ACTIVITY BOX

1 This sentence has been written without any vowels in it.

Th r r nly tw nty n l tt rs n th s lph b t

Can you read it? Write down what it says.

2 How many different words can you make by adding vowels to these two consonants?

c t

(Answer: act, cat, coat, cot, cut, cute, acute)

About 3 000 years ago in Phoenicia (Lebanon), a scribe or school of scribes replaced syllabic writing with something completely new – an **alphabet** with about 22 single signs for single sounds. But they didn't invent letters for all the vowels. Their language wasn't hard to read without vowels. (Some languages, like Hebrew and Arabic, don't always write vowels today, and people can still read the writing easily.) This was a huge advance in the history of writing.

But then the ancient Greeks, who traded with the Phoenicians, saw what a good idea the alphabet was and they borrowed it. In Greek, they needed to write vowels or their words became very hard to read. So they started to use some of the letters for vowel sounds. By about 2500 years ago they had signs for all the vowel sounds.

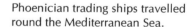

Phoenician trading ships travelled round the Mediterranean Sea.

Α α	alpha	Η η	eta	Ν ν	nu	Τ τ	tau
Β β	beta	Θ θ	theta	Ξ ξ	xi	Υ υ	upsilon
Γ γ	gamma	Ι ι	iota	Ο ο	omicron	Φ φ	phi
Δ δ	delta	Κ κ	kappa	Π π	pi	Χ χ	chi
Ε ε	epsilon	Λ λ	lamda	Ρ ρ	rho	Ψ ψ	psi
Ζ ζ	zeta	Μ ..	mu	Σ ς	sigma		omega

This Greek writing on a statuette of a lyre player says 'Deliches dedicated me'

Later, the Romans adopted the Greek alphabet. They made some changes to suit their language, Latin. When the Roman emperors conquered most of Europe they took their writing with them. Today people who speak English or Western European languages all use the Roman alphabet, though we have added some letters.

M·IVNIVS·M·L
HAMILLVS·SIBI·ET
IVNIAE·PIERIDI
CONIVGI·CARISSIMAE

A Roman funerary inscription.

Other scripts, like Arabic and many in India, developed from Phoenician writing too but they became quite different.

Arabic script.

The reason why the alphabet was so important was that it is quite easy to learn twenty or thirty signs for sounds. Before, it took years of special training to learn the hundreds of different pictograms or syllabic signs. Now many more people can learn to read and write, and people can communicate information

ACTIVITY BOX

1 The following alphabets were developed by different groups of people living in the areas marked on the map. The numbers on the map will help you to find out which.

Write the name under each alphabet.

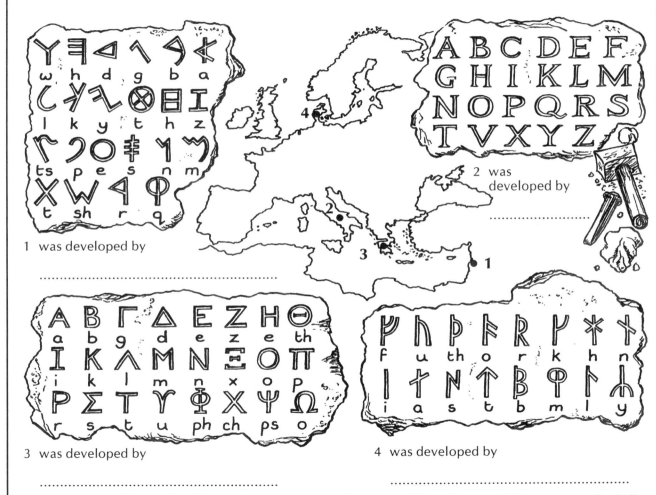

1 was developed by

....

2 was developed by

....

3 was developed by

....

4 was developed by

....

2 Choose one of these alphabets and write some words in it (try WASHINGTON). You may not find all the letters you need.

Complete this sentence:

In the .... alphabet, my name is spelt ....

The reasons we write, the people we write for

There can be many different reasons for writing. We might need to record events and information. We might wish to sign our name or to give written instructions.

We might write to many different people (different audiences) at home and at school.

Signatures
Many rulers had very elaborate signatures.

Queen Elizabeth I's signature

Each Ottoman Sultan had an elaborate signature called a **tugra**. It was used on coins, buildings and documents.

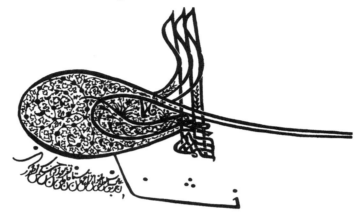

Spells and curses
Spells and curses have been written many times in the past. This one was written on an Egyptian heart-scarab. It is Spell 30 from The Book of the Dead.

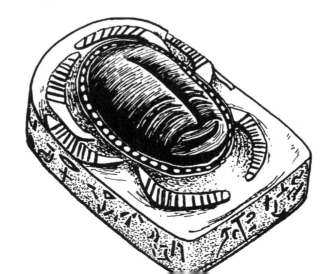

Writing for decoration
The Arabic script of the Islamic world is used both for writing and for decoration. Pictures of people or animals are not allowed in mosques, so the walls and other objects are decorated with the beautiful patterns formed by their script.

ACTIVITY BOX

1 Design your own tugra or special signature. Use coloured pencils or, even better, paints or inks. You could make the first letter very large and use a shortened version of your name.

2 Get some thick string, a piece of stiff cardboard about 7cm square and some strong glue. Now draw the first letter of your name in capitals on the card, cut the string to fit the letter shape and glue it down on the card. Use some thick paint to soak the string and then print your letter pattern carefully as many times as you can on a clean sheet of paper.

How were children taught to write in the past?

Often in the ancient world, only boys had lessons, not girls. Not every boy learned to write, either. Poor children didn't, and even rich people might use a trained scribe rather than learn to write themselves.

A hundred years ago, in Victorian times, it was still true that very few people could write. Only the wealthier people were well educated.

Even today the majority of people in the world cannot write. There are still differences between boys' and girls' education in some countries, too. For example, in Japan boys and girls use different scripts and have to use different words for the same thing.

ACTIVITY BOX

1 At school you might sometimes copy from a handwriting book to try to improve your writing style. This type of book is not new. Children all the way back to Mesopotamia or ancient Egypt also had to do this task.

Here is a handwriting manual from about 100 years ago.

Copy some of the handwriting out on the lines underneath.

Give yourself marks out of ten for your work!

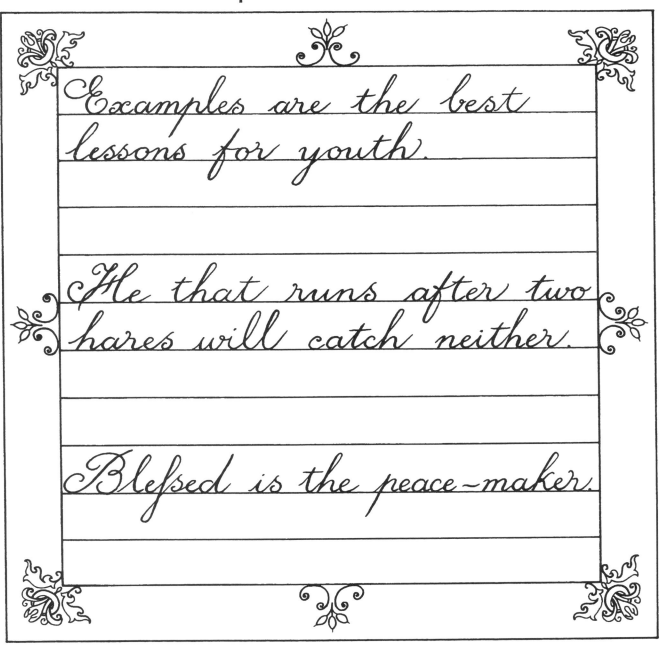

Examples are the best lessons for youth.

He that runs after two hares will catch neither.

Blessed is the peace-maker.

How can writing help us to find out more about the past?

In 1973, archaeologists unearthed 200 Roman writing tablets at the fort of Vindolanda near Hadrian's wall. The tablets were probably written during the twenty years before the original building of the wall in AD122. They are the oldest written documents to be found in Britain.

The letters tell us what the soldiers wore and what they ate. One reads 'I have sent you ... a pair of socks from Sattua, two pairs of sandals and two pairs of underpants ... '

Another tablet listed the following food supplies 'spices, roe deer, salt, young pig, ham, wheat, venison ...'

Join the dots to complete this picture of a Roman soldier guarding Hadrian's wall.

Writings of long ago are one of the many clues that we can use to find out about the past. Sometimes **archaeologists** make wonderful finds with large numbers of **artefacts**. In other cases they only find a few things. The Diamond Sutra (see page 14) is the earliest dated printed book – it is in Chinese and is a Buddhist prayer. We don't know how many other books like it there were. Often we are unable to discover the whole story!

The tablets were made of thin pieces of wood approximately one third of the size of this page. The tablets were written in Latin and are mainly letters, food lists and other accounts. Each tablet was attached to another by punching holes in the edge and tying them together with cord. The tablets were then folded in a concertina shape to form a package and bound with cord.

When the tablets were found, many of them were damaged or incomplete, so the archaeologists had to guess some missing words.

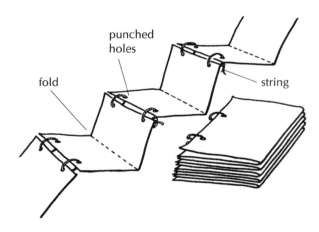

fold — punched holes — string

ACTIVITY BOX

1 Make a folding letter of cardboard and string like the wooden tablets found at Vindolanda.

2 Decide what to write on your tablets. You could invent a list of supplies for a modern army, or a recipe book, or a supermarket shopping list. Think about how it should look. What other food lists can you think of?

3 Use a dictionary to find and write down definitions of these words: ARCHAEOLOGISTS, LATIN, ARTEFACTS.

Cracking the code

The secret of hieroglyphs

On page 4 you read about Ancient Egyptian hieroglyphic picture writing.

The meaning of these pictures was a secret until a large slab of black stone with writing on was discovered by French soldiers in Egypt in 1799. This famous slab is known as the Rosetta Stone because the soldiers found it in a village called Rosetta.

On the stone was writing in three different scripts: Greek, Demotic and Ancient Egyptian hieroglyphs. Demotic writing was a simpler, 'everyday' kind of hieroglyphic script, which developed from the earlier Hieratic (see page 4).

As the Greek script could be understood, many people tried to decipher the hieroglyphs by matching them to the Greek words.

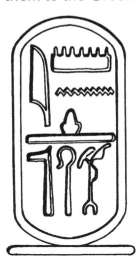

You can find the Rosetta Stone in the British Museum and see for yourself how difficult the writing is to read and why it took such a long time to crack the code!

A Frenchman, Jean-François Champollion, finally managed to translate the hieroglyphs in 1822, by studying a small number of words which had an oval line drawn around them. This line, called a **cartouche**, was drawn around the name of the rulers. Champollion recognised the names of Ptolemy and Cleopatra in the Greek script and some letters were found in both words. By matching up the hieroglyphs to the Greek letters in the words he knew it was possible to begin the long process of deciphering hieroglyphic writing.

The secret of the hieroglyphs had been

ACTIVITY BOX

1 Work with a friend. Make up your own code using any symbols you want – you could use numbers, letters or even your own signs. Start by putting down all the letters of the alphabet and your chosen symbols underneath each letter. Keep all this secret at this stage!

2 Write out the name of someone in your family and their address – don't tell anyone the information yet! Swop the coded name and address with your partner and see if he/she can crack the codes. If one of the codes is very, very simple he/she might be able to guess at it, but that's unlikely!

3 Now give each other the names and addresses and a short coded message to decode. It should be easier this time!

Indus Valley script

Experts are still trying to decipher the script of the Indus people of Northern India and Pakistan. The writing appears on carved stone seals, pottery and bangles. Archaeologists think the words on the seals may be the names of people who used the seals to mark clay tags. The tags were tied onto valuable goods that were traded far away. Where else in this book have you read about clay tags?

What changes did printing bring to people's lives?

Before printing was developed, the only way to produce a book was to write it out by hand. Just imagine writing out your favourite book! You can see that it took a long, long time to write out books and it was a very expensive way of making them.

Printing was first developed in Asia, well over 1000 years ago. Korea may have been the first country to print large numbers of copies of Buddhist prayers as long ago as AD 704. The roots of modern printing in Europe were in the 15th century, about 500 years ago.

The Diamond Sutra

The earliest forms of printing in Asia were made with woodblocks and were used to print Buddhist charms or prayers.

The Diamond Sutra is the earliest dated printed book in the world. It is a Buddhist prayer printed with woodblocks on seven sheets of paper glued together to form a scroll. It was found in a cave in China at the beginning of this century. We know when it was made because the date appears in the text – it's dated 'the 15th of the 4th moon of the 9th year of Xiantong', which is 11th May 868 by our calendar.

ACTIVITY BOX

1 Use some stiff card and a piece of wood to make a printing block – use the block to print the title of a scroll book. Remember to reverse the letters so that they print the correct way.

2 Now make the book in scroll form. You need to find the right sort of paper and glue so that your book will roll up.

Cut out the card letters. Glue them on to the wooden block – the wrong way round!

Ink the letters using oil-based ink and a roller.

Cover the block with a sheet of paper. Press or rub it down evenly.

Carefully remove the paper and let the ink dry. Now write the rest of your book!

A page from the Gutenberg Bible, and examples of the illuminated letters and borders which decorate the book.

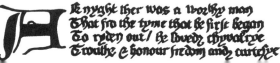

The Gutenburg Bible

Wooden blocks had made printing possible, but the carving of letters or a whole page still took a long time – and it was expensive. The idea of movable type was invented by the Chinese in the 11th century AD. In Europe it was invented 400 years later by a German, Johann Gutenberg. Movable type consisted of single letters on small metal blocks that could be set into words and sentences and re-used many times.

The Gutenberg Bible was printed in Germany in 1455. It is a huge book with over 1,200 pages in two volumes.

Caxton's Canterbury Tales

The technology of printing spread throughout the rest of Europe and arrived in England in the late 15th century. William Caxton set up the first printing press in Britain, at Westminster Abbey. He printed the first edition of Chaucer's Canterbury Tales. He printed a second version in 1483. This time, he corrected the script and added pictures. Caxton managed to combine both old and new ideas about printing as the words were printed using the new movable type but the pictures were still printed using wooden blocks.

What will happen in the future? Will we still need to write?

Technology has changed most people's lives over the last twenty years. Keyboards and computers are now common in schools and offices where only pencil and paper were previously used. Some forms of technology can be voice activated. CD ROMs create colourful, moving and talking computer encyclopaedias. Printing has been revolutionised by desk-top publishing and we can find out information easily using not only books but also CD ROM, television and the Internet.

© 1996 The Trustees of the British Museum

Published by British Museum Press
A division of The British Museum Company
46 Bloomsbury Street, London, WC1B 3QQ

ISBN 0 7141 1762 5

Designed and developed by Fieldwork Limited,
61 Gray's Inn Road, London WC1X 8TL

Drawings and back cover illustration by Patricia Hansom. Front cover illustration by Peter Dennis.

Printed in Great Britain by
St Edmundsbury Press Ltd,
Bury St Edmunds, Suffolk

The past – 100 years ago.

The present.

The future – 100 years from now?